PROFORÇA THEATRE COMPANY & THE LION & UNICORN THEATRE PRESENT

LATELY

BY JAMES LEWIS

Published by Playdead Press 2023

© James Lewis 2023

James Lewis has asserted his rights under the Copyright, Design and Patents Act, 1988, to be identified as the author of this work.

A CIP catalogue record for this book is available from the British Library.

ISBN 978-1-915533-11-1

Caution

All rights whatsoever in this play are strictly reserved and application for performance should be sought through Proforça Theatre Company before rehearsals begin. No performance may be given unless a license has been obtained. Please contact via Proforça Theatre Company, C/O Theataccounts, 1 The Oakley, Kidderminster Road, Droitwich, Worcs, WR9 0AY. Or by email to hello@proforca.co.uk with the subject - LATELY - PERFORMANCE RIGHTS.

This book is sold subject to the condition that it shall not by way of trade or otherwise, be lent, resold, hired out, or otherwise circulated without the publisher's prior consent in any form of binding or cover other than that in which it is published and without a similar condition including this condition being imposed on the subsequent purchaser.

Playdead Press
www.playdeadpress.com

CAST & CREATIVES [2023]

Callum / Cal	Fred Wardale
Alison / Alf	Lauren Ferdinand
Callum's Dad	Ross Kernahan
Callum's Mum	Demelza O'Sullivan

Lately was originally performed in September 2021 at the Lion & Unicorn Theatre, Kentish Town, Produced by **Proforça Theatre Company**. The original cast were:

Callum / Cal	Fred Wardale & Matt Wake
Alison / Alf	Lauren Ferdinand & Gabrielle Nellis-Pain

FOR PROFORÇA THEATRE COMPANY

Written by: James Lewis
Directed by: David Brady
Movement / Intimacy Director: Lucy Glassbrook
Dramaturgy: Georgie Bailey
Associate Director: Jess Barton
Casting Director: Suzy Catliff
Show Technician: Rose Hockaday
Lighting / Sound Design: Proforca Theatre Company
Public Relations: Matthew Parker
Additional Marketing: Terri Paddock – MyTheatreMates
Legal Services: Alletsons Solicitors
Accountancy Services: Theataccounts
Consulting Producer: Antony Stuart-Hicks
Videography: ChewBoy Productions
Production Mascot: Eddie

FOR THE LION & UNICORN THEATRE:

Artistic Director: David Brady

Operations Manager: Dodie Finamore

FOH Duty Managers: Nance Turner, Jakey Newton, Carli Green, Grace Gjertsen, Georgie Bailey, Joe Rose & Melina Gary.

The Producers Wish To Thank:
Marian & John Brady, Anthony Fagan, Vicki Marsh, Vicki Macgregor, Phil Daley, Hannah Daniels, Catrin Bailey-Jones & Paris Bailey-Jones, Harriet Lambert, Erin Read, Melissa Phillips, Matthew Webb, Emma Burnell, Kim Scopes, Miriam Duignan, Claire Bourke, Olivia Thompson, Everything Theatre, Heather Jeffrey & London Pub Theatres, Kieran Doherty, Jack Albert Cook, The Associate Artists of the Lion & Unicorn Theatre 2019-2022. Henry Brackenridge, Sarah Rickman, Hal Darling, David Meredith, Kevin Shaw & the Albany Theatre Coventry, Young's Pubs & everyone who else who has supported *Lately* on its journey.

Lauren Ferdinand | Alison / Alf

Lauren trained at Rose Bruford & The National Youth Theatre. Lauren is an Associate Artist of Proforça Theatre Company.

Previous work includes originating the role of Alf in *Lately* (Lion & Unicorn Theatre, Albany Theatre, UK Tour 2023). Previous Theatre credits include Alex in *Before Feel* (Lion & Unicorn Theatre). Other work includes; *Best Served Cold* (Leicester Curve); *White Millionaire Emmas*; *Ghosts* & *Cleansed* as well as Sophie in *Volcano* & Shanice in *Flashbang*.

Fred Wardale | Callum / Cal

Fred is an actor from the East Midlands who graduated from Royal Birmingham Conservatoire. Fred is an Associate Artist of Proforça Theatre Company.

Previous work with the company includes originating the role of Deano in the critically-acclaimed *Flashbang* and the original, Offie-nominated run of *Lately*.

Fred has worked on various short films and voiceover projects. He is also a writer, regularly creating his own material, with his first play currently in the works.

James Lewis | Writer

James Lewis is a critically-acclaimed writer based in London. Previous credits include *If I Go* (2016), *Feel* (2018/19, UK Tour), *Reading Gaol* (2017/18), *At Last* (2019), the critically-acclaimed *Lately* (2021, UK Tour), *Volcano* (2022) and *Flashbang* (2022). James also contributed the pieces *Charlie* (2018), *Georgie* (2019), *Ryan* (2020) and *Euan* (2023) to Proforça's *Feel More* anthology companion to *Feel*.

James's work has been performed at the Lion & Unicorn Theatre, King's Head Theatre, The Space, Theatre N16,

Albany Theatre Coventry, Upstairs at the Western, Town & Gown Cambridge, Ye Olde Rose & Crown Theatre, Hertford Theatre, Laurels, the Alma Theatre & the Old Joint Stock Theatre.

David Brady | Director
David is an Offie-Nominated Writer, Director, and Artistic Director from Coventry based in London. For Proforça credits include; *If I Go* (2016), *Saucy Jack & The Space Vixens* (2016), *The Importance of Being Earnest* (2017), *Reading Gaol* (2017-18), *Feel* (2018-19), *Feel More* (2018-2020), *At Last* (2019), *AAAAA [FiveA]* (2021) and the Offie Nominated *Lately* (2021 & UK Tour 2022) & critically-acclaimed *Flashbang* (2022).

Other credits include; *Getting Rid* (2018) for Actor Awareness, work for Far Cry Theatre (2019), Hooked Theatre (2022) and Associate Producer of *BLUEBIRD* (2018) and *2nd Coming Again* (2018-2019). He has directed work at YORAC, Theatre N16, The King's Head Theatre, Hertford Theatre, Upstairs at the Western, The Alma Theatre, The Space, & The Albany Theatre Coventry (amongst others).

David is also the Artistic Director of the Lion & Unicorn Theatre in Kentish Town and was awarded a special commendation for services to Pub Theatre in 2021 by London Pub Theatres Magazine.

Lucy Glassbrook | Movement & Intimacy Director
Lucy is a Movement Director and choreographer, working with small casts on stories with brilliant storytelling. As a creator she is inspired by encounters with people from all walks of life, drawing inspiration from the communities the stories live within. She works with intimacy guidelines and

her creation process journeys through embodied understanding and creating a culture of respect.

Her recent work includes; *Lately*, *Volcano*, *Flashbang*, Coventry City of Culture Opening Ceremony and *Fighting Irish* at The Belgrade Theatre and the Opening & Closing Ceremonies for the Commonwealth Games.

Georgie Bailey | Dramaturgy
Georgie Bailey is an award-winning Playwright and Poet. In 2020, he graduated from Bristol Old Vic Theatre School's MA Dramatic Writing and recently completed his tenure as one of the Oxford Playhouse Playmakers. He's an alumnus of Soho Theatre, HighTide Theatre and Papatango's respective playwright development schemes and won the Innovative Play Award 2021 from London Pub Theatres, whilst receiving 2 OFFIE nominations last year for projects he worked on. Georgie is the co-Artistic Director of the critically acclaimed, award-winning multi-arts company ChewBoy Productions.

Recent credits include: *TETHERED* and *Volcano* (both Lion and Unicorn Theatre); *The Prang* (Bristol Old Vic Theatre School); *DJ Bazzer's Year 6 Disco* (Golden Goose Theatre, Riverside Studios); *These Things That Burn* (Broken Silence Theatre); *Tadpoles* (Bristol Old Vic Theatre School); *GORGER* (Oxford Playhouse Extract) and *The Waters of Brygstow* (Unreal Estates Bristol).

PROFORÇA THEATRE COMPANY

Proforça Theatre Company is a critically-acclaimed theatre company based in London. It is our mission to create great theatre experiences which challenge, entertain, and confront our audiences.

Proforça Theatre Company was founded in late 2015. In addition to running a theatre company designed to promote and support the work of writers, actors, and directors through the creation of brilliant new fringe theatre work. We're also the managing company in charge of running and programming The Lion & Unicorn Theatre in Kentish Town.

Since 2016 we've presented new pieces of writing such as *If I Go* and the critically acclaimed and very successful expanded universes of *Feel* and *Feel More*, *Volcano & Flashbang* as well as new takes on exciting work such as *The Importance of Being Earnest*, a compelling fusion of original text and new writing in a remix of *Reading Gaol*, & the musical *Saucy Jack & The Space Vixens*. We have a reputation for high quality, high integrity fringe theatre which champions and showcases the talents of emerging creatives of all kinds.

We work hard to make sure that we operate with high standards of integrity and stewardship, and ensure that we take the utmost care of everyone we work with. We are commercially savvy and exceptionally well organised, and are starting to build some great relationships with venues and other companies outside of the London area, which we hope to continue to build as we embark on future projects. We believe this gives us an advantage and something unique we can offer over other theatre companies in the capital.

We try to create a "Proforça" way of doing things, not only within the company, but in making partnerships and supporting other performers, companies and artists. We're part of a fantastic network of London theatre-makers, and we love being a part of such an amazingly creative group of companies, talented individuals, and fully embrace the role we play in the fringe theatre community.

Website: www.proforca.co.uk

Social Media: @proforcatheatre

LION & UNICORN THEATRE

The Lion & Unicorn Theatre is a 60-seat black box studio theatre based above the Lion & Unicorn pub at the heart of Kentish Town, with Camden Town just a stone's throw away.

The venue is led by Artistic Director **David Brady** and provides a great home for the best in fringe theatre talent that London has to offer and we are keen to provide a warm, nurturing, and brilliant experience for both theatre makers and audiences alike.

In addition, the theatre supports new writing, and provides opportunities for a team of Associate Artists which includes a brilliant cross section of London fringe theatre creatives.

Since **Proforça Theatre Company** assumed responsibility for operating the venue in March 2019 we have not only developed a reputation for programming new and exciting work from some of the best theatre makers in London, we've made the venue both profitable as well as re-establishing the theatre as a destination fringe theatre venue with most productions in our inaugural seasons winning critical acclaim and award nominations.

The Lion & Unicorn Pub offers a brilliant pre and post show experience, with premium beers, wines and spirits as well as a fantastic and varied food menu offering great pub food. For a night of culture and excellent hospitality, there is no better place to spend an evening than at one of London's most well-respected pub theatres.

We are always looking to develop and enhance our creative partnerships, and we welcome any discussions about future reciprocal touring arrangements which may enhance our ability to support producers who may be interested in supporting the theatre for other projects. We have a vibrant and viable asset which other theatre companies are not necessarily able to offer prospective producing partners and are keen to promote these opportunities in 2023 and beyond.

Website: www.thelionandunicorntheatre.com

Social Media: @landutheatre.

Lately is dedicated to Fred, Lauren, Matt and Gabrielle.

Thank you for being my mate. x

CHARACTERS
CALLUM (CAL) – 21, M
ALISON (ALF) – 21, F

CALLUM'S DAD (VOICEOVER), Fifties - M
CALLUM'S MUM (VOICEOVER), Forties – F.

A NOTE ON PLACE & TIME
The action takes place in a non-descript seaside town, somewhere in the UK, over the period of one year. Accents and locations can vary.

The show can be staged as simply as you like. We used projections and two concrete blocks – but like it is for Callum and Alison, Shithole-on-Sea can be whatever you make of it.

CONTENT ADVISORY
This play contains very strong language, adult themes, discussion of sex & sexual activity, discussions of bereavement and suicide.

For more information, advice and support with any of the issues raised in this play, please visit **Samaritans** (www.samaritans.org) or the **Campaign Against Living Miserably (CALM)** (www.thecalmzone.net)

THE END

The sound of the sea.

CALLUM (CAL) sitting centre stage.

As he starts speaking he lays out (almost precisely) in front of him is his wallet, keys, mobile phone with tape round it and a battered pair of Converse trainers.

ALISON (ALF) is in the background somewhere.

He thinks for a minute. Like this is difficult to say.

CAL: I don't know where to start.

Not really.

Thought it would be simple. Come here, say some stuff. Lay it all out and leave everything behind.

But it's not easy. Is it?

Smiles a bit.

Always knew we'd end up by the sea. You and me. Always thought this was the furthest place we could go, and now it's real isn't it? Looking at the waves and wondering what happens next.

Hoping that all of this will make sense to someone. Maybe to you if not to me.

Pauses for a second.

I'm sorry. I never meant to hurt anyone, least of all you.

> I just hope that maybe it I take this opportunity to explain, that you'll understand.

ALISON (ALF) fades into the foreground. She looks down at the stuff he left behind, like it's after the event.

ALF: I don't know how this is going to end.

> Not really.

> Can't believe I missed you.

> Got here six weeks too late and now all there is left is pieces to pick up.

> Fuck's sake, Callum.

> Like properly, fuck's sake.

She looks down at his stuff. Picks the things up one at a time. Gathering everything.

> I think about you sometimes. Not all the time, obviously, because that would be weird. Just sometimes.

> Just sometimes, when it catches me out.

She holds onto his stuff. Pulls it close.

> I just wish somehow that you could help me understand.

TRANSITION

HIM & HER

She puts his stuff to one side. Keeps going. There's a lighting change.

ALF: *(Smiling)*

Got asked the other day how we met.

Had to think a bit really, because its all like some weird blur. Redacted.

He just sort of drifted. Faded in like a an old fashioned photograph.

Turned up one day at school in like Year 11 or the Sixth Form or whatever and nobody really knew how he got there.

Been inside my head ever since.

CAL: Tried to find the right word for her.

Intimidating?

Nah, that's not it.

Impressive. Yeah. Let's go with that.

Smiling

She'd got everything clear in her head. Like it all made perfect sense all the time - Always had a smart answer for everything…

ALF: You know there's always some kid that turns up in one of the later years at school? They always carry round that sense about them that they've missed too much, always playing catch up to fit in with the rest of us?

Well that. He never shook it off. Not once. He was always kind of on the outside, looking in.

Looks across at him. Smiles.

Dunno why I liked him, but I did.

Might have been his smile. Might have been the way he wasn't like all the other boy racers that seemed to pop up round here. Might just have been he wasn't a dick.

Might just have been the look in his eye he got sometimes. The one that you'd catch sometimes when you knew there was more going on under the surface.

CAL: She didn't give a shit. Not about anything. Or at least that's what it looked like. Always challenging people. Asking why. Wanting to get out and see stuff. The world, whatever. Never taking no for an answer.

And she was like, a lot you know? If I'm honest - particularly for someone like me who wasn't.

Proper agent of chaos. The sort of person who'd chuck a pound coin into the penny arcade machine to see what would happen, just to see if it would fuck up the system.

He smiles a bit, cheeky. To her.

Actually you were a proper nightmare.

ALF: *(Interrupting)* Er - No I wasn't.

CAL: Yeah, you were.

But you were brilliant. You are brilliant, I mean. It's just that no-one ever told you that you're sort of terrifying, at least at first.

ALF: Now I think about it, I'm not sure if anyone actually ever fitted in here anyway. We were all just sort of thrown together and made the best of it. You just sort of found people you didn't hate and hung onto each other.

My Mum used to compare him to a bit of driftwood – when she was in one of her romantic moods and I didn't have the energy to tell her to shut up because she was embarrassing.

Thoughtfully.

But she was right, actually. He just sort of washed up on the beach. One day he was just there and that was it.

CAL: One day was enough for us to become well, whatever we ended up being. Wasn't it?

And he looks at her and smiles.

TRANSITION

SHIT PARENTING

Callum and Alf – Separate spotlights. Looking across at each other. Together yet separate.

CAL: Guess you could say we were both the products of shit parenting.

Money, jobs, most things that required the ability to function successfully as a capable human being.

We moved around a lot - One house to the next every time they ran out of cash. Random blokes banging on the door all hours of the day and night. One pay day loan to another.

ALF: We weren't that special either, by the way. Be nice to say we were but no.

Mum and Dad hated each other too, in the end. She's a bit of a hippy and he used to run the used car dealership on the Coast Road. Recipe for disaster.

Married for fifteen years till he has some sort of midlife crisis and announces on their wedding anniversary he's been shagging some other woman.

She's over this story already.

It would be funny if it wasn't so pathetic.

CAL: …The only time they spoke to each other was when he used to get home battered at Stupid O'Clock and they'd start yelling at each other…

ALF: All passive aggressive in our house. Mum frantically bleaching all the work surfaces in the kitchen over and over, Dad hiding in the garage tinkering with some ridiculous heap of junk he'd bought from some auction somewhere...

CAL: ...Proper screaming matches. Shouting over Match of the Day. Slurring the worst kind of things that you could only say to someone that you really loved or really hated.

Never knew which it was. Just used to listen from upstairs and hope that it would all be over soon...

ALF: And it's fine now, whatever. Boring from the car dealership shacking up with Debbie from the Nail Bar. Ridiculous.

At least I know where I get the running away from.

CAL: Wasn't always just yelling. Sometimes it would be proper fights. Throwing stuff, punches mostly.

Falling asleep hiding in the duvet while the people you think you love take chunks out of each other downstairs...

He gives it a second.

Yeah, that was proper fucked up, that was.

On Callum.

ALF: I used to look across at him, occasionally. Some Monday mornings and there'd be a black eye. Scratches on his arms or whatever. Bruises in strange places.

She looks across at him. He suddenly becomes self-conscious, like she can still see him.

CAL: - It's fine, Don't worry about it. Got battered in the park with some mates at the weekend. Fell over on the way home.

ALF: Stopped asking. We knew what was going on. You could all see it.

CAL: Doesn't hurt, it's fine. Nothing to worry about. I'm just a twat for falling over.

ALF: Now I'm not saying he needed protecting. I just don't know how you could do that to someone else, no matter how bad it got.

Nobody deserves that.

I dunno how he put up with it for so long.

Pause. Take a breath.

CAL: There was this one Saturday, evening, out of nowhere, my Mum had enough. Told him he was on his own and to fuck off or whatever – Packed up what she had and moved out.

Just remember her slinging what clothes she could find into a bin bag.

He didn't even go far to chase after her – He'd had a skinful. I just remember him wheezing names at us from the porch steps as she got into a minicab.

She took the only money she could grab and never looked back at him.

Or me.

Not once.

We never talked about her after that.

ALF: He never really talked about her. Never knew where she went, just somewhere far away.

CAL: Just left me and him. Stuck in that house which was never clean and cold all the time. Him getting sicker all the time.

Stops a minute to push away the memory.

Properly shit.

ALF: Barry from *Barry's Autos* moved with Debbie from the Nail Bar on my Seventeenth birthday – *Cheers Bazza, nice one.*

Came home from school and my Mum's in the kitchen pretending there was nothing wrong. Fajitas for tea.

Oh I should probably mention Debbie had this white Fiat 500 which she was really proud of. Used to drive round town with fake plastic eyelashes on her headlights.

CAL: Did She? Really? Eyelashes? What a twat.

Alf just looks at him. Eyebrow.

ALF: Baffles me to this day why he would do that? Leave your wife for someone with half a brain and way too much fake tan, let alone fuck off forever and never come back.

Why would you do that to your kid?

Proudly. Confides a secret.

Stuck a screwdriver into her tyres a few weeks later.

CAL: Fucking brilliant. What did your Mum say about that?

ALF: Who do you think passed me the screwdriver?

CAL: Fair enough.

Change of subject. Back to Callum.

ALF: Maybe it was that we'd both been fucked up by our respective family situations. Maybe we just collided at the right time.

CAL: I dunno – Maybe the universe was conspiring to push us together for some reason. I like to think, anyway.

There's a shift back again, leaving Alf back on her own.

ALF: Yeah? Well fuck that. The universe has got a shitload to answer for.

TRANSITION

THE KRAKEN

An angry man shouting and coughing. Callum's Dad calling from a room elsewhere in their flat. Drunken raging – distorted sounds. Bleak and dark sounding. (Voiceover / blackout).

DAD: *Callum!*

A cough interrupts a longer cry for attention.

Callum!

The blackout lifts. Callum sat on his own, somewhere centre stage.

CAL: I remember when I was little, there used to be this library book at school. One of those picture books for small kids. Myths and Legends, that sort of thing.

And the cover of that book is this ship, one of those old school sailing boats. Masts and oars. It's got these massive tentacles wrapped round the boat.

And that picture is like nothing I've seen. It's all angry blues and greens and purples. Sailors in the water and they're all crying out and drowning as this monster crushes the boat into tiny splinters.

Used to fascinate me, that picture. Used to wake up at night with nightmares that the creature was going to get me. That the monster was going to emerge from under my bed and drag me into the dark with its suckers. This terrified little boy being dragged under the water.

Another shout, strangled with coughing.

DAD: *Why won't you come help me – you lazy little bastard.*

CAL: Got told I was stupid. Got told to be quiet when I cried, so I learned to stop. Eventually.

Fear never went away though. Never shook the feeling there was something coming out of the dark to get me, one day.

His Dad again, meaner and more evil this time.

DAD: *You were always useless. You wonder why she fucking left you? Just like everybody else...*

Callum – as if responding with fear to the voice in the next room...

CAL: Always knew that monster would grab hold of me in the end.

The monster always wins, doesn't it?

TRANSITION

CANDY FLOSS

Warmth. Light & Colour. A funfair on the pier. Reds and oranges as the sun starts to go down. The sounds of the rides in the air.

CAL: You know you get that one night in the year where it's just like, I dunno, like –

He mimes "ok"

End of a steaming hot day and the world just sort of, breathes out a bit?

The sound of the funfair in the background gets louder.

We used to have those sometimes. Sun goes down and everyone's out enjoying themselves. Even if it's just for a few hours.

Yeah, they were the best times, really.

Families. Kids. Eating too much sugar and trying not to kill themselves on that catapult thing or make themselves sick on the waltzers.

Thoughtfully.

Mums and Dads laughing. Everyone having a good time.

Alf – looking at candy floss in a bag. Like it's a scientific curiosity. Interrupts.

ALF: This stuff, never really understood it.

CAL: *(To audience)* Well most of us, anyway.

(To Alf) What do you mean?

ALF: Well it's completely pointless, isn't it? It's most of the other stuff here. Just this wedge of whipped up pink shit. Short term solution designed to make you forget your problems.

CAL: I mean, you could just, like, calm down and eat it maybe?

ALF: Or... I could just keep most of my teeth and not die of diabetes, thanks.

She puts the bag down.

CAL: What did you buy it for then?

ALF: I didn't, that bloke that runs the sweet stall gave to me. Jasmine's Dad. The one with a hook for a hand.

CAL: Oh come on. Jasmine's Dad does not have a hook for a hand.

ALF: Yeah he does. I'm telling you. Passes this bag of shit candy floss over to me, looks me up and down, says "*Alright darling, you should smile more*" and then winks at me. Prick!

CAL: You're the worst.

ALF: No. Jasmine's Dad is the worst. I mean, someone should tell him he's running the wrong stall, because I know for as fact that there's another stall over there with a load of ducks bobbing about with nobody to like, you know...

She sarcastically mimes "hooking a duck."

At least it would be a distraction from his wandering eyes I suppose.

She shrugs. Bored.

CAL: We don't have to stay here you know, we could go somewhere else if you're bored?

ALF: Are you kidding? Where else is there to go? This is literally all there is, and its properly shit. Other people get to go out clubbing, I'm sat on a Saturday dodging the sleazy attentions of Captain Fucking Hook.

CAL: I'm changing the subject. You should too.

I dunno – we could go into town. Get something to eat. Go to the cinema or something?

ALF: Oh, Hold on a minute while I contain my excitement.

CAL: …Or we could just stay here instead? You could take out some of your frustration on that "Test Your Strength" machine..?

ALF: Do you really think giving me a hammer is a good idea?

CAL: Fair point.

Pause. Thoughtful.

It's not as bad as you make it out to be.

ALF: (*Continues*) Are you kidding? Look at it. This whole town is a shithole. Theatre burned down years ago, restaurants closed, shops on the high street boarded up. Betting shops full of drunk old blokes. Sad old ladies waiting in wind-battered shelters for buses that never come.

I mean come on, even Wetherspoons gave up on us.

CAL: But it's home though. Closest I ever came to one, anyway.

Besides. Who gives a fuck about Wetherspoons?

ALF: What I'm saying is that the problem with living here is that everything is just a little bit shit. Isn't it?

This might have been somewhere once. You know? Romantic even. Lights from the prom bouncing off the seafront and the sound of kids laughing. The smell of fish and chips on the wind.

But it's fucked now, isn't it? Those dodgems have been broken for as long as I've been alive and those donkeys look like they belong in rehab.

CAL: I think it's kinda beautiful, most of the time. Nowhere else like it.

ALF: Nah. Shithole-on-Sea. Fucking hate it. You couldn't pay people to move here.

CAL: We did.

ALF: Yeah, well you've always been an exception to the rule. Proper weird, you.

CAL: Awkward.

He looks at her.

ALF: Sorry. You know what I mean.

Holds his hands up. Forgiveness.

CAL: I just think you're a bit kind of harsh on it all the time. You never really give it a chance.

He takes the bag of candy floss of her. Takes a piece and starts eating while she's talking. Realises its gross halfway through.

ALF: You reckon?

CAL: Yeah.

ALF: Well the day I give it a chance, my friend, will be the day that I give up. Decide to give in and open a candy floss store on the pier. You can find me between Captain Bluebeard over there and that catapult ride that keeps threatening to kill everyone.

Nobody's ever going to write a story about what goes on here. Far Too Boring.

She looks at him.

And why are you making that face?

CAL: Because you're mad, you are.

And this Candy floss really is shit, isn't it?

ALF: I did say.

CAL: Come on. Let's get out of here. You've got me thinking about fish and chips now.

He gets out his wallet. Waves it at her.

> I'll even buy them, this time, if you want.

Pause. Almost flirtatious.

ALF: I think...

Hold for anticipation.

> That's the best idea you've had all day.

And he smiles and the two of them head off together as the sound of the funfair gets louder.

TRANSITION

FIREWORKS

Late night. The two of them standing on the beach together. A few months later. Fireworks in the background or in the sky behind them.

CAL: Every year there used to be this big sort of festival thing. Beginning of October, just as it was starting to get cold. Council used to throw this big party. End of the season thing. Hot dogs, Jacket potatoes. Everyone watching the fireworks on the beach.

Fireworks underscore the next lines. Intercutting or interrupting the dialogue.

ALF: Running joke in our house that the festival happened to coincide with my birthday, so when I was a kid my Dad used to make me think that they'd put the fireworks on specially for me. Birthday party on the beach for his little princess.

One more disappointment when I found out they weren't actually for me. *Cheers Dad, Nice one...*

CAL: She *hated* her birthday. Another one of those pointless days where everyone made a fuss. Once watched her walk away from a group of people singing *"Happy Birthday"* to her because she never liked surprise parties.

ALF: It wasn't the party, it was the surprise. Far too extra. And the singing.

He goes to step in but she interrupts.

- And the people actually. *Especially* the people.

CAL: ...Cake and everything. Candles. Very Awkward.

ALF: Oh who gives a fuck? If nothing else this was just an excuse. Making out it was some massive treat to go out and stand in the freezing cold whooping like idiots at some gunpowder going off.

CAL: No birthday presents. Not ever. That was the rule. So every year, we did this instead.

Big firework. They watch it burst above them and the action moves back to them looking up at the sky...

ALF: Not doing this next year.

CAL: What do you mean?

ALF: This. Standing here. On this beach. For my next birthday. Not doing it.

CAL: As you're so fond of saying – what else would you do instead?

ALF: Fair point, but I mean it. Not planning on being here next year. Nope.

CAL: So where are you going to end up instead?

ALF: Dunno. Doesn't matter. Going to be anywhere else but here. Alaska, Argentina, Australia. Somewhere beginning with an A. Somewhere you need to get on a plane to visit.

CAL: Err. Financially that's going to be interesting. Let me know how that goes, yeah?

ALF: If you want something badly enough then it'll happen.

Pause. An offer.

> You could always come with me?

CAL: What?

ALF: Come with me. Chuck a few things in a bag and let's go.

CAL: That's mad. Who does that?

ALF: Me. I do that.

CAL: I dunno Alf. Things at home. Besides. Why would you want me hanging round with you?

ALF: Because we spend enough time together. And let's be honest you're sort of the only person who I can tolerate most of the time.

Would get you away from here for a start.

CAL: Never really thought about it like that.

ALF: Well you should. Think about it I mean.

CAL: The thought of just doing that. Running away like that with no planning. Sort of terrifying. Who can see that far into the future anyway?

ALF: Well right now all I see is fireworks.

CAL: Funny. No, like thinking ahead. Making plans. Wishing for something that you want to come true. That's not how it works. Can't just leg it.

ALF: Well you know what I wish for.

Can't believe there's nothing you want.

CAL: I dunno – never have done. Close my eyes and all I can see is *blank*. Never really wanted for anything much. Never really wanted anything.

ALF: Don't be daft, of course you do.

CAL: Nope. Not a thing. It's like I close my eyes and instead of seeing kids, or family, or this happy life somewhere like some people can, all I can see is this black void. The things that other people want I don't. Like I don't ever see them happening for me.

Don't see anything. Not even a firework.

Another firework goes off over them.

ALF: Well, Fuck it, and fuck that. Get a job in a bar, Work the summer. Save up some money and come with me. Easy. Next year we could be on the beach in Thailand.

CAL: Oh come on, it's never that easy. You know it's not.

Besides. Thailand doesn't begin with an A, does it?

ALF: Look, it doesn't matter. Just promise me next year you won't be here. You won't be stuck in that house with that person who makes your life a nightmare, and you'll find something else. Something better.

Has she said something out of turn?

He looks away.

Sorry – That came out harsher than I thought.

> I'm sure he loves you really.

CAL: You reckon? I'm not so sure.

She doesn't reply immediately.

> Yeah don't answer that, actually. I know exactly what you think.

ALF: I mean it Callum. You can do so much more. You deserve so much better. You should live a life you make for yourself. Not one that you're forced to live in by someone else.

> Just think about it. Yeah?

There's another big firework. He pauses a moment. Looks at her.

CAL: Alf?

ALF: Yeah. What?

CAL: Time to change the subject now.

ALF: If you want.

CAL: Happy Birthday.

And he turns and kisses her on the head as a large burst of fireworks bloom above their head. The two of them, standing in the dark, looking up at the sky...

TRANSITION

BLANKET

The two of them are half sitting, half lying side by side on the floor, under a blanket. Beach hut somewhere. Undressed. Bottle of beer each. It's clear they've just slept together.

Callum's watch is off to the side somewhere.

CAL: Thought we said we weren't doing that again?

ALF: What?

CAL: That. You and me. *That.*

He indicates the bed. Them.

This.

ALF: Well we say that and we keep doing it. So.

CAL: So.

ALF: So, I don't mind if you don't.

CAL: I don't mind, no.

Kisses her. Swings his legs round out of the blanket. Goes to get up and put his shirt on. Looks for his trousers. She watches from a distance.

He's got bruises on his ribs. Old ones and new ones. Scratches. Signs of a recent fight.

ALF: Going to talk to me about them?

CAL: About what?

ALF: The bruises. Not blind. Bit difficult to touch someone when they keep wincing all the time.

Self conscious. He's uncomfortable.

CAL: It's nothing. Don't worry about it.

ALF: But I do. Genuinely. That's not normal.

CAL: You just used to it. He has a bad day, I have a bad day. It all kicks off, then you pick up the pieces and move past it. Don't you?

ALF: No Cal, you don't. You shouldn't have to "move past" it. Wanker.

CAL: Look, it is what it is. Just have to get on with it. He can't help it. Nobody else to help him.

ALF: Well that's bullshit and you know it. No excuse. Like being trapped in a locked room with a cobra.

CAL: Guess you stop worrying about it after a bit and accept it. Just life, isn't it. Used to it.

ALF: Well that's not right. Going to kill you dead.

CAL: He's not going to kill me, don't be dramatic. It just is what it is.

Besides, something happens to him and I'm fucked. Right?

ALF: Not really. You'd be happier for a start - Not being a human punchbag -

Interrupts

CAL: He doesn't mean to do that either. He just lashes out sometimes when he's frustrated.

Look, can we change the subject? I think I preferred what we doing before -

ALF: Why? Why are you afraid of talking about it?

Snaps a little bit.

CAL: Because I can't change it. Alright?

She holds her hands up. Eyebrow goes up. Hit a nerve.

They sit for a few seconds. Awkward. He looks at the beer bottle.

I just think there's other things to be afraid of. Bigger things. I suppose.

ALF: What do you mean by that?

CAL: I dunno. Loads of stuff. Getting old, North Korea lobbing bombs across the ocean, everyone dying in a pandemic, panic buying toilet paper. Donald fucking Trump.

All that stuff which seems ridiculous until you realise that the world's actually turning to shit and we're all going to die.

ALF: We're not all going to die, Cal.

CAL: But how do you know?

ALF: Because the universe has a way of, I dunno – like fixing itself or whatever. You can always change things. Things aren't inevitable.

CAL: Aren't they?

ALF: Course not. you don't have to accept the hand you're given all the time.

You can change the future, if you want to.

CAL: Ok then, if you're going there. What are you afraid of?

ALF: Oh I dunno, loads of stuff. Losing my mind, not recognising my family. Getting old, marrying an estate agent called Dennis and ending up like my Mum.

Maybe I'm just scared of the word "forever".

CAL: Forever? Bit deep.

ALF: It's this big scary immovable object, isn't it? Take your eye off the ball. Stop planning and the next thing is that you're stuck here and that's it.

Next thing you know you're married with kids and resenting the fact your husband is spending too long in the garage working on the car. Again. Watching another coachload of pensioners disappear into the sunset year after year.

That sort of "forever" The permanent one. No Thanks.

Callum thinks for a minute, before offering...

CAL: Did you ever have one of those big nights out? Nightclub or whatever. Hundreds of people all bouncing up and down. Singing, dancing, sweating, all that stuff.

In that minute it's probably OK, isn't it? Shared experience, like you're all in it together.

I've never had that. Never got that connection. Not with anyone. Like there is this thing that they all can do that I can't. Means I'm never going to find a place that fits.

Never found a place where it all comes together.

ALF: I don't get what you mean.

CAL: What I mean is that it feels like I'm missing something.

Worried I'm going to end up like my Dad instead. Dragging himself round his shithole of a flat. Wheezing out every last breath. Nobody noticing I'm gone until someone sounds the alarm because something doesn't smell right.

ALF: Well that's grim. Isn't it?

CAL: It's not even thinking it. It's living it. Dad decides he's had enough and gives up and dies or whatever and then what?

She shifts and looks at him. Thoughtful.

ALF: Then you adapt. Keep going. You make your own choices, Don't you? Things can always change.

CAL: But what if this is the last chance? Like you've met the last person or are in the last place that you'll ever be happy? What if you fuck it all up?

ALF: I think you can spend time worrying about the worst things that are going to happen and they never actually do, do they? Spend all that time worrying and not enough time living.

She reaches over. Grabs his watch and his arm and puts the watch on for him.

Not for me.

He goes to get up, but changes his mind. Kisses her on the head. Gets back under the blanket and gets closer to her again.

Besides, what the worst that could actually happen anyway?

He just looks at her. Hangs onto her for reassurance as the lights go down.

TRANSITION

PADDED ENVELOPE

Alf on her own.

ALF: So the night of my birthday my Dad turns up. Hovers on the doorstep. Looking over my shoulder in case my Mum decides she's not having it and starts another pointless row.

Can't stop long. He says. *Sorry – Debbie is at home waiting.*

Shuffles about. *Wanted to say Happy Birthday.*

Reaches into his pocket. Present for you, he says. Thought you might want to go on holiday. Get on a plane or something.

Eyebrow raises. Pause a minute.

What do you say to that without sounding like an ungrateful twat? *Er thanks a lot Dad, but instead of your guilt money I'd have preferred it if you hadn't walked out on us for a nail technician with pink hair extensions half your age instead?*

Don't worry, I didn't say that.

Pauses. Pulls it back a bit.

Five grand. Notes in a padded envelope.

Looks for a word.

Transactional – That's what it was.

> *Just make sure it's a return ticket, you know, in case you get into trouble or whatever. Be safe.*

And it's the most awkward thing ever. Like he was handing over the cash for one of his dodgy used motors in a car park to his mate Derek. Like he's collecting something he bought off a stranger on eBay.

She shrugs.

We make small talk. I say thank you. He kisses me on the head, gets in the car and drives off. See you in a few weeks then.

Five Grand in a padded envelope. And that's enough to get to Thailand isn't it? Even escaping feels a bit underwhelming round here.

Confessional. Pauses a second.

I meant to say something. Find the time. Sit Callum down and say I was going. Do it properly.

But when do we actually do anything properly round here anyway?

To Callum.

I always meant to make the time and explain. I promise. It just never happened the way I wanted it to. There was always something got in the way.

I was going to explain. It's not like it was a secret.

But then the shit really did hit the fan...

TRANSITION

SHIT HAPPENS

Alf in the dark. Dimly lit, like it's night. She's got her phone with her.

ALF: I guess I should have seen it coming. The signs were there I suppose.

Bad news on the horizon. It was always on the way.

We used to talk. Hours. Middle of the night. Didn't matter whether we were together or not. You can put the world to rights with all-inclusive minutes.

Hours in the dark.

But then he sort of went quiet for a few days. Didn't seem right. Didn't think about it at first. Guess we had other stuff on. He's busy or whatever. Sent a few texts with no reply. Got on with stuff.

Then a few nights later-

Sound of a text message. She looks at it. It's from him. She doesn't say what it says.

Spotlight. Callum. Immobile. Something wrong.

I look out the window and he's just standing there. Outside the house, In the dark.

And it's like he's shut down or something. Standing there in the freezing cold. He's barely registering.

She goes towards him.

What the hell is wrong with you?

He doesn't answer. He just looks at her.

She's worked it out already.

    Oh shit. Oh Callum –

The next bit is fragmented. Like he doesn't know what he wants to say or it comes out in the wrong order.

CAL: He's gone.

ALF: What do you mean gone?

CAL: Stroke. He had a stroke.

    Came home and found him in bed. Wouldn't wake up.

    Wouldn't answer the door. Had to break the door down.

ALF: Jesus.

CAL: Didn't know what to do. Didn't know who to call. Couldn't leave the house. Didn't want to leave him, not really. In case he woke up, I mean.

    So I just sat there. With the body. Which was stupid - Because he wasn't going to wake up. Was he?

ALF: What the fuck. Why didn't you call anyone?

CAL: I dunno. Didn't know who.

    Sat there for two days.

    Even held his hand at one point.

ALF: Fucking hell, Callum. But he's not still at home now, right? Please tell me he's not still there…

CAL: No, No, it's ok. The neighbours came. Ambulance came and took him away. It's all being sorted now. Funeral is next week.

Just sat there looking at him. Looked like a completely different person.

And he just looks at her, lost.

ALF: Fuck. Callum. You should have called. My Mum would have done something. Called someone for you. Anything.

CAL: It's OK. He's gone now.

Autopilot.

Can I stay with you, please?

ALF: Yes. I mean yes of course. Of Course you can.

He sort of looks round in a daze.

CAL: Fuck.

I don't know what to do.

And he goes over to her and he hangs on to her for dear life as she stands there.

ALF: Neither do I.

And he breaks down into her and sobs as the light goes.

TRANSITION

CORNFLAKES

Alf. On her own. Spotlight.

ALF: Fuck me, it was grim. Like actually one of the worst things ever, watching that. He just sort of was. For hours, days at a time. Shut down. Grey mode.

Sat through that funeral. Could only have been ten of us there. Watching the world's most pathetic coffin disappear in through the curtains to get incinerated.

And I'm watching Callum that whole time knowing he's on his own. Him sleeping in my bed like some sort of rescue animal. Watching him in free fall. Telling him when to eat, when to have a shower. Dodging annoying questions from my Mum when she wonders why I've basically got a random mate of mine living in my bedroom living off Cornflakes.

Knowing that everyone's left him was hard.

Knowing I'm about to join that list of people in a short while is worse.

Pause. A bit defensive.

Like I said, there was never going to be a right time. We just did what we could.

TRANSITION:

VOICEMAIL

The light changes. Callum and his phone. It's covered with tape. Smashed screen. He picks it up and fiddles with it. Voice message tone.

Callum's Mum. She's not read the room properly.

MUM: *(V/O)* Hello love. It's Mum. I'm sorry I haven't been in touch for a while but you know how it is. Life just gets in the way sometimes, doesn't it?

I heard about your Dad. I'm sorry love. Now I don't want to speak badly of the dead but he was a wanker wasn't he? Look at it this way, like I said you before. You've got to get away, haven't you? If it's not right I mean. Find a new start if it doesn't work out for you and try again. That's what I did anyway. Best decision I ever made. But I'm happy now, I think. Whole new life, brand new opportunities. And you can be too now! You can get away now you're not looking after that useless idiot anymore.

You could come here, you know, few days away might do you good after all that trouble. Although probably not for too long, yeah? We don't have that much space and you know what work's like. Actually maybe best you don't really. I don't think you'd like it here.

I'll call you in a few weeks I suppose.

See you soon love. Bye!

Back to Callum. He ends the message. Looks at his phone. Lost.

TRANSITION

A DIFFICULT CONVERSATION

Callum and Alf. Sitting by the sea.

Difficult conversation. She's told him she's leaving.

Awkward silence.

CAL: How long have you known?

ALF: Does it matter? Since my birthday, A few weeks after. Dad gave me this cash and I booked the tickets.

CAL: Well we all know that you wanted to go.

ALF: Yeah? Well I'm not going to apologise for that. You know I'm not.

CAL: I just thought-

ALF: Thought what? Callum? That I'd give up and stay? Not fucking likely.

Look, it's not personal. I just need out of here. Away from all of this. It's killing me dead.

Too close to the mark.

I'm sorry. I didn't mean it.

CAL: Yeah we know what you mean.

ALF: The offer's still there. You could always come with me? Do you good. Get some sunshine.

CAL Don't think I'm cut out for Thailand somehow.

ALF: Could be a whole new start.

CAL: But what if I don't want a whole new start, Alf? Everyone saying the best thing for me to do is to fuck off somewhere when everything I have is here.

Everything is all fucked up now. Isn't it?

ALF: I'm sorry Callum. You know I am. This trip. It's my chance. It's everything I've always wanted.

CAL: I'm not sure you are. Sorry, I mean. Because if you were then you wouldn't go.

That hit a nerve.

ALF: Oh *fuck. off.* Don't pull that - That's not fair.

CAL: Oh I think if the last few weeks have taught us anything we're way past fair.

He holds for a minute. Calms a bit.

Maybe you're right.

ALF: I'm sorry. I don't know what you want me to say? I've made my mind up. I'm going.

I don't want you to feel this is because of you, or about you. This is about me, because it has to be. And I'm sorry, I've not no fucking idea who we are or what we are to each other, but I know I've got to do this, for myself.

CAL: And how do you know you're coming back? You'll just keep moving on.

ALF: Because we know this place. Everyone always does.

Things will be better by then, I promise - and we'll just see how it goes. Yeah?

CAL: But do they really? Get better I mean?

Ask yourself honestly though, what have you really got to come back for?

She looks back at him. Honest as ever, and thinks about it for a second. perhaps a second too long before she offers him a very small but very meaningful shrug.

TRANSITION

HAPPY BIRTHDAY

Callum and Alf - Separate parts of the stage. Eight Hours and 6,000 miles away from each other. They can't see each other.

ALF: Legged it. Course I did. Always said I would.

Smashed as much as I could into that trip. Full Moon parties on the beach, and riding on the back of elephants like some massive fucking cliché. Getting wasted, kissing random Australian boys on the promise of them taking me to ride horses on a ranch in the outback. Getting up and doing whatever I wanted.

CAL: Just sort of drifted after she left. Didn't know what else to do. Gave up any hope of finding a job. Didn't seem to be any point. Not really.

Used to walk. Head down. Point myself in the direction of somewhere. Didn't matter where.

Used to walk past the pubs in town, orange light spilling out onto the pavement on a Saturday night. People inside laughing, dancing, swaying to music with their mates. Looking like they were having the best time. Me standing on the pavement looking in, even if it rained.

Stops a minute. It's too painful.

Yeah, I stopped doing that after a bit.

ALF: Hanging out with those people taught me so much, you know? About being free and not following the rules. Not giving one ounce of a shit.

Except there's this nagging feeling like I've left something, OK, somebody behind. It's there in my head the whole time like some nagging mosquito bite that I want to scratch.

CAL: It was like everything else went into freefall. Sometimes I'd just get battered. Bottle of vodka to pass a few hours. Sit down the other end of the seafront where nobody really ever went. Lean myself against the wall and get wasted till it wouldn't matter anymore. Close my eyes and wish it to be done with.

ALF: Turned 22 on the beach in Koh Samui. I just needed to take a day, like just one day away from getting shit-faced with all those randoms just to sit, you know? Take it in. Watch the sky, mediate. whatever.

I sit there, four in the morning on this beach watching the sun come up, and all I can do it think about you - were you OK?

Six thousand miles away and all I can think about is this place. Drives me insane.

A firework goes off, somewhere. Explodes.

CAL: End of the season party, just like last year. Except is isn't it? Because everything's different now. Kept thinking how it was your birthday and wondering what you were doing.

And in the background I'm watching all these fireworks going off, but it's like someone's turned off all the colour.

ALF: I'm sat watching the most beautiful sunset I've ever seen, all on my own, and I couldn't take it. It just made me so angry for you, about you, because of you.

And I hate you a little bit for that. I really do. Because there's a part of me that feels like you fucked it. Screwed it up, for both of us.

Pushed it away. Not for the first time either. I was mad and angry at you because here I was trying to see how big the world was and all you could do was to see how small you could make it.

CAL: I know I didn't regret not going. Because I couldn't.

I know that it never felt right to leave here and go with you, but on the other hand I didn't know what to do now.

Looking around and everything you thought you knew, took for granted, whatever, wasn't there anymore.

ALF: Running away was supposed to be the answer, right? I'd either come back older and wiser and ready to get on with my life or just not come back at all because I'd have found something better.

And she laughs a bit, bitterly. Because it's absurd.

That fucking tractor beam always pulls you home. Doesn't it? Even the sunrise in Thailand can't compete with Shithole-on-Sea.

CAL: Out of the corner of my eye somewhere I can see this little girl with her Dad. She's on his shoulders looking at the fireworks. They're both laughing, making the most of every minute.

And in that moment I think about all those things that I never knew I wanted. Kids, Family, making a life together. Wanting but never having.

It won't come together. I'm never going to have those things. Am I?

ALF: A few weeks pass and like the end of every holiday, it was time to come home, wasn't it?

Shit happens.

You have have to give it all up to come back here. Slinking home with your tail between your legs.

CAL: That's when I realise that I know what it is. That thing that's been coming for me all this time out of the dark. It's all been leading up to this moment, isn't it?

ALF: The cash is all spent, and all that's left is a tattoo I'll probably regret in 3 months time, a dirty suntan, and a broken phone full of memories of a time when the world felt like it was better, and there was another place that wasn't here.

CAL: It all comes crashing in, crashing down, whatever. Like some angry wave in a thunderstorm rolling in off the sea. Out of the sea and onto that beach where I'm standing.

The worst feeling ever.

ALF: Plane lands at Heathrow, the wheels hit the tarmac which is greasy with rain, and all I can think about is that there's nothing here for me anymore.

CAL: And it hits me like a hammer. Mum running away, Dad dying. Never being able to make any of it work.

Pause for a second.

I'm completely on my own.

ALF: I go through Arrivals and of course my Dad's busy so Debbie picks me up at the airport and the two of us sit there in that fucking car of hers. The one with the eyelashes. And we say barely a word to each other, just sitting there, and I can tell she's just dying to say something.

I think for a minute that she probably looks at my Mum the same way. Both of us losers together.

I don't know what you think you won Debs, because this doesn't feel like first prize to me.

CAL: How do you get out of that? Dead End. All makes sense at last. Running away to the sea to escape because that's the furthest you can go. But it isn't. Is it?

ALF: And as we pull up in the driveway she makes some below-the-belt comment like I should get a proper job now that "I've gotten it out of my system" or whatever it was. Tidy myself up and get my nails done properly. Get a proper job. Stop being such a massive disappointment.

She reacts.

> I wanted to put a brick through her stupid windscreen. Tell her to fuck herself, maybe.
>
> But I didn't do either of those things.

CAL: Just wanted to walk right there and then into the ocean. Let it take me. Leave everything behind. Find some way to make everything not hurt anymore...

ALF: She was right though, wasn't she? This place had taught me a lesson, made me learn my place in the world, yanked me back and told me that it was time to grow up.

To Callum, angrily, like she's been able to see him all along.

> And you wonder why I hated it here?

And there's a look, across all the miles and spaces between them as the lights go down and the space is plunged into the dark.

TRANSITION

THE BEGINNING

The sound of the sea.

Callum (Cal) sitting centre stage.

As he starts speaking he lays out almost precisely in front of him is his wallet, keys, and a battered pair of Converse trainers.

Allison (Alf) is in the background somewhere.

He thinks for a minute. Like it's difficult to say.

CAL: I don't know where to start.

    Not really.

    Thought it would be easy. Come here, say some stuff. Lay it all out and leave everything behind.

    But it's never that easy, is it?

He smiles.

    It's just that lately, well, it won't come together you know? Can't make it work, no matter how hard I try.

    The bruises you can see might be gone. Not so sure about the ones you can't.

Takes a deep breath.

    Always knew we'd end up by the sea. You and me. Thought I'd reach the beach and that would be as far as I could go.

    Now I guess we'll find out how much further the waves can take me.

>Sorry, I'm an idiot. I hope this all makes sense, to you, if not to me. I never meant to hurt anyone, least of all you.
>
>And I don't want you to be feel sorry for me. Please, because I don't know if I could handle that. Not really. All I know is that everything hurts too much and now if I do this then it's all going to be OK. Isn't it? It's nobody's fault – I just can't do this anymore.

Offers this, from somewhere.

>You know, you said once that nobody would tell a story like ours – Like nobody would be interested? This little town. Our story.
>
>I just thought that if I did then maybe you'd understand. Even if I can't tell you myself anymore.
>
>The monster always wins. Right?

The last line of the note.

>Thank you for being my friend.

And he takes off his shirt, folds it neatly in front of him, and then out of his pocket takes a letter. Their story, everything he wanted to say.

He moves quietly into the background, leaving the pile of his stuff behind. Just like in the beginning.

Alf picks up his letter, clear now that this is the story she's been reading all along.

ALF: I don't know where this is going to end.

Not really.

Can't believe I missed you.

Six weeks too late and this is everything that's left.

Fuck's sake, Callum. What a mess.

She looks down at his stuff. Picks the things up one at a time. Gathering everything. Including the letter. It's clear this is where it's all been headed.

I think about you sometimes.

Not all the time, obviously, because that would be weird.

Just sometimes, when I get caught out.

Random, odd moments when you least expect it. I'll just be somewhere and then you'll just appear, like that lost kid that washed up here all those years ago like a bit of driftwood.

Drives me insane.

The light changes. Callum in a golden warm light on a summer afternoon.

I'll go down the beach on a Sunday afternoon, just as the sun is going down and all those bloody tourists are driving off in their coaches and I think I see you sitting on the wall by the beach in the distance.

Hiding in the shadows in the sunlight or the reflection on the water, like a mirage.

But that's shit and romantic and ridiculous. Because it was never like that. Was it?

Boys on the street with sad eyes. Battered old pairs of converse trainers. Unexplained bruises on a Monday morning.

Sometimes I'll smile and keep going. Sometimes I'll just do that thing I always do. Shake my head and tell myself off for being so fucking stupid for seeing things that were never there in the first place.

Sometimes I get angry. That happens a lot, actually. Really fucking angry at you. Because you were loved, Callum. You really were. And then I realise I'm a hypocrite for telling you off for taking the easy way out when that's all I ever wanted to do.

She looks over at him. Briefly.

So cheers for that, mate. Nice one.

But then it passes. The tide goes out, the anger subsides or the light changes or whatever and it's not really a daydream anymore.

And it makes me so sad. All those things that could have been. All those things you could have found for yourself.

The waves roll in or the tide goes out or whatever and the memory of you fades away. Just for a little bit at least.

The light goes out and he disappears as the sea takes him and he's gone.

Pause a minute.

> Anyway, thought you should know. I've made some decisions. Big ones, actually. Found myself a job in Birmingham - tried to get as far away from Shithole-On-Sea as possible. Not sure there's anything left for me now.

Laughs a bit, sadly.

> Here's hoping that it's for forever this time.

Stops a minute.

> Just wonder how much of ourselves we'll leave behind.

The last line of the note. She reads.

> Thank you for being my mate too.

And she picks up the pile of his stuff, including the suicide note, pulls it close to her chest, just for a second, before leaving the circle and heading out there, somewhere.

And the light fades on her the sound of the sea gets louder again.

Stage fades to black.

CURTAIN